ELVIS PRESLEY

" QUOTE UNQUOTE "

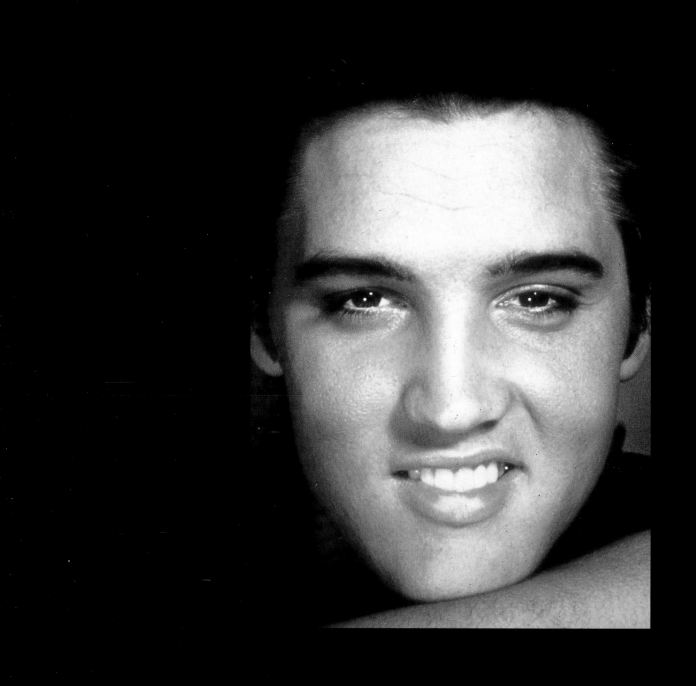

ELVIS PRESLEY

" QUOTE UNQUOTE "

Arthur Davis

CRESCENT BOOKS
NEW YORK • AVENEL

ACKNOWLEDGEMENTS

The author and publisher acknowledge the following references,
where many of the quotes in this book can be found.

Jerry Hopkins, *Elvis: A Biography*; **Jerry Hopkins**, *Elvis: The Final Years*;
John Tobler and **Richard Wootton**, *Elvis: The Legend and the Music;*
Red and **Sonny West, Dave Hebler** and **Steve Dunleavy**, *Elvis: What Happened?*;
Richard Wootton, *Elvis Presley, King of Rock and Roll.*

PICTURE CREDITS

Camera Press page 57; **Ronald Grant Archive** pages 26, 31, 66; **London
Features** front cover, pages 38, 69; **Pictorial Press** back cover, pages 2, 6, 9,
11, 12, 13, 14, 18, 19, 21, 22, 37, 39, 44, 46 right, 48, 54, 58, 59, 60, 65, 76,
79; **Range/Bettman/UPI** pages 24, 30, 32, 35, 36, 46 left, 47, 53, 63, 72,
73, 74; **Redferns** page 50; **Redferns/Stephen Morley** page 70; **Rex
Features** pages 17, 40, 45, 56, 67, 68; **Rex Features/Doc Pelé** page 28.

This 1995 edition published by
Crescent Books, distributed by Random House Value
Publishing, Inc.,
40 Englehard Avenue, Avenel, New Jersey 07001.

Random House
New York • Toronto • London • Sydney • Auckland

A CIP catalog record for this book is available from the
Library of Congress

Publishing Manager: Sally Harper
Editor: Barbara Horn
Design and DTP: Crump Design

ISBN 1 85813 836 1

Printed in Italy

CONTENTS

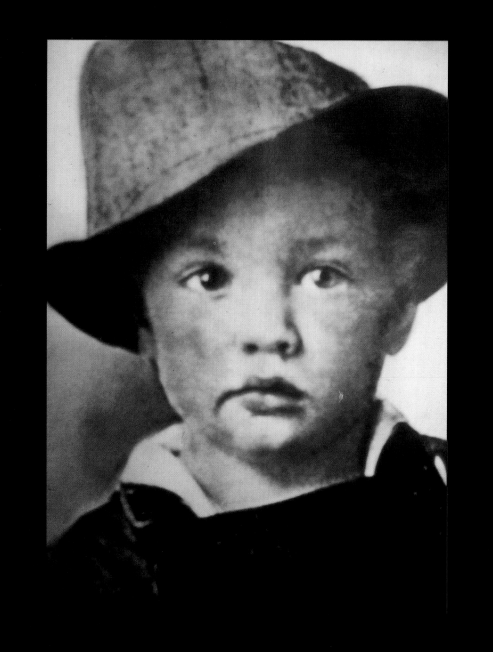

BORN IN MISSISSIPPI

'Since I was two years old, all I knew was gospel
music. During the singing in church, the
preachers used to cut up all over the place —
that's how I was introduced to the onstage
wiggle, because the preachers did it.
The congregation loved it and I remember
one day a preacher jumping on a piano.
I guess I learned a lot from them.'

FACING PAGE: *Elvis Presley had an impoverished childhood, only enriched with
the music he heard at the local Pentecostal church.*

UNTIL HIS UNTIMELY DEATH, Elvis Presley was the King of Rock 'n' Roll, acknowledged as such by The Beatles, who dominated the 1960s just as he had the 1950s – as John Lennon said, 'Before Elvis, there was nothing, and without him, there would be no Beatles.' Born in Tupelo, Mississippi, on 8 January 1935, to Vernon and Gladys Presley, who lived in a two-roomed wooden cabin and were far from rich, Elvis had a twin brother, Jesse, who was stillborn, which Elvis later blamed on the family's impoverished situation.

'My little brother died, and my mama almost died, because we couldn't afford to go to hospital.'

Perhaps because of the death of one baby, Gladys Presley, who was twenty-three when she became a mother, tended to spoil her surviving son. Elvis went everywhere with his over-protective mother, sometimes to his considerable embarrassment. Despite this, he led a fairly normal childhood,

---

'My mama never let me out of her sight. I couldn't go down to the creek. Sometimes when I was little, I used to run off, so Mama would whip me and I thought she didn't love me.'

---

attending school as an average pupil, but shining only once, when he was eight years old. After a teacher heard him sing 'Old Shep', a sentimental song about the death of a dog, Elvis was entered in a talent contest at a state fair, and won second prize, five dollars and as many free rides as he wanted that day. However, his only musical progress for many years thereafter was his regular attendance at the local Pentecostal church, where he absorbed deeply the sounds of gospel music – and the exuberant gyrations of the preachers, which he claimed was the origin of his famous wiggle.

Being unable to keep up payments on their modest house, the Presley family was forced to move in with Vernon Presley's brother, Vester, and his wife, Cletis, who was Gladys's sister. The first guitar Elvis ever played belonged to his Uncle Vester,

and when he was given a less battered instrument for his birthday (instead of the bicycle he wanted, which his parents could not afford), he became attached to it, learning to play it alongside music he heard on the radio.

He enjoyed gospel music best, but he also got to like country music (then known as 'Hillbilly') and the blues, the musical form created by black people in America. Vernon and Gladys didn't approve of 'black' music, calling it sinful and dirty, which was the way many Southern white people regarded it at the time, so Elvis had to listen in secret to the music that became the roots of his style.

To the Presley family, the development of musical styles was utterly irrelevant at this time: their only aim was to survive, an

LEFT: *Gladys Presley doted on her son, while Vernon tried to persuade him not to follow his musical ambitions.*

'We were broke, man, broke, and we left Tupelo overnight. Dad packed all our belongings in boxes and put them on the top and in the trunk of a 1939 Plymouth, and we just headed for Memphis.'

increasingly difficult problem as Vernon Presley's prospects of getting regular well-paid work decreased from rare to extinct. In 1948, when Elvis was thirteen years old, Vernon reluctantly decided that he and his family should move to Memphis, 'the big city'. Few people knew of their departure and probably fewer cared when the Presley family vanished.

When they arrived in Memphis, Elvis was unhappy about his new hometown. The first accommodation the family found was woeful: a single room without any cooking facilities, and a bathroom they had to share with several other families in similarly dire straits.

Elvis wasn't keen on Humes High School either, although Gladys's insistence on walking there with him was obviously embarrassing for the teenager, and he later complained that Gladys was still taking him to school when he was fifteen! Eventually, he settled down, and began to develop his apparently dormant interest in music, although it came as a shock to Mildred Scrivener, a teacher at Humes High, that this seemingly average pupil possessed considerable talent.

Life slowly began to improve for the family. They could afford to pay the rent on a two-bedroom flat after Vernon found a job at a paint factory and Gladys went to work at a local hospital, and even Elvis contributed by mowing lawns for money. This upward trend was short-lived, for Gladys suffered from regular ill-health and had to stop working. Elvis was forced to find an evening job to supplement the family income, and his resultant lack of sleep led to his nodding off during school lessons. One of these jobs was in a cinema, from which he was fired for watching films when he

'I never knew Elvis could sing until someone in my class said Elvis should bring his guitar to our picnic. While everyone else was running around, Elvis sat quietly by himself playing and singing to the few around him. Slowly, other students began to join them — there was something about his plaintive singing that drew them like a magnet.'

MILDRED SCRIVENER,

A TEACHER AT HUMES HIGH SCHOOL

should have been showing customers to their seats. Among the movie stars who particularly impressed him was Tony Curtis, whose pompadour hairstyle Elvis began to copy during his final years at school in the early 1950s.

This dramatic change of appearance became an obsession for Elvis, almost leading to violence on one occasion until a timely intervention by his friend Red West, who rescued him from jealous classmates determined to trim his crowning glory. A grateful Elvis later gave West a job for many years as his companion and bodyguard.

In 1953 Elvis left school and went to work as a delivery driver for the Crown

BELOW: *Elvis in the bedroom of his Memphis home, 1954.*

'*If he had had a regular haircut like the rest of us, he probably wouldn't have been bothered, but I guess the other kids thought he was trying to show off or something. I have never known any other human being take more time over his hair. He would spend hours on it, smoothing it and combing it.*'

RED WEST ON ELVIS'S HAIRSTYLE

Electrical Company. It was hardly a top job, but it was one that allowed him to move around and consider his future, which did not seem especially promising. Vernon scorned his son's musical ambitions, on the basis that he himself knew several guitar players and few of them worked regularly. He told Elvis he must choose between

becoming an electrician or a guitarist, adding the rider that 'he'd never seen a guitar player that was worth a damn'.

During the second half of 1953 Elvis Presley's career as a singer began, although falteringly, when he decided to record a couple of songs for his mother's birthday. The Memphis Recording Service was operated by Sam Phillips, an ex-disc jockey who

LEFT: *Elvis always took a particular interest in his appearance, copying the hairstyles of stars such as Tony Curtis.*

'When I was driving my truck, and one of them big shiny cars went by, it started me to day-dreaming. I always felt that someday, somehow, something would change for me. I didn't know exactly what, but it was a feeling that the future looked kinda bright.'

made private recordings, such as messages from servicemen to their families. Before long, Phillips also found himself in demand for recording local functions, which provided enough business to allow him to indulge his own interest in black music. During the early 1950s the Memphis Recording Service studio was used to record a number of local black musicians, the most famous of whom were B.B. King, today the godfather of the blues guitar; soul legend Rufus Thomas and Ike Turner, who later married a girl named Annie Mae Bullock, better known as Tina Turner.

Phillips also operated a small independent label he called Sun Records. The first hit on Sun was 'Bear Cat' by Rufus Thomas, which was a musical response to and spoof of 'Hound Dog' by Big Mama Thornton. This was somewhat ironic, as three years later the same song performed by Elvis, would top the US chart for eleven weeks and sell a million copies.

And that might never have happened if Elvis had not been heard by Marion Keisker, Sam Phillips's secretary. Marion had been impressed by Elvis's vocal ability, which in 1954 led Phillips to invite Elvis to record a song that he had been sent by a music publishing company. The results were less than spectacular, but Phillips saw Presley's raw talent, and introduced him to two local musicians, guitarist Winfield Scott 'Scotty' Moore and double-bass player Bill Black. It is at this point that the story of Elvis Presley really begins.

RIGHT: *Performing in the mid-1950s with Bill Black on bass and Scotty Moore on guitar.*

SUNSHINE IN MEMPHIS

'I was doing a show in Memphis and I came on-stage and was scared stiff. I did a fast-type tune, and everyone was hollering, but I didn't know why. When I came offstage, my manager told me they were hollering because I was wiggling.'

Scotty Moore, who had never met Elvis before, was surprised by the young vocalist's appearance, but he and Bill Black didn't allow first impressions to colour their judgement. After a couple of hours playing

---

'He was wearing a pink suit, white shoes and a ducktail [hairstyle], and I thought my wife was going to go out of the back door!'
Scotty Moore on the first time he saw Elvis

---

mutually familiar songs, Moore was sufficiently impressed to tell Sam Phillips that Elvis could sing well enough, and that if he recorded the right song, anything was possible. Phillips encouraged the guitarist and bass player to continue rehearsing with Elvis, and in July 1954, decided to allow them studio time to attempt a recording. They ran through several songs they had rehearsed, but Phillips was unimpressed. The sentimental country songs he was hearing seemed too polite.

After a while Elvis and the musicians decided to stop for coffee. This was one of the most significant pauses for refreshment in music history, as Scotty Moore recalled: 'We were having a break, and all of a sudden Elvis started singing a song, jumping around and acting the fool, and then Bill picked up his bass and started acting the fool too, and then I started playing. Sam had the door to the control booth open and he stuck his head out and said "What are you doing?", and we said we didn't know, so he said "Well, find a place to start and do it again".' What Elvis had started to sing was 'That's All Right'. Presley, Moore and Black played it with more urgency than the original recording, moving the song away from a deliberate blues style and towards rhythms more often associated with country music, and creating an exciting fusion of black and white musical styles. To Phillips this seemed to be exactly what he had mentioned to Marion Keisker: a white boy who could sing like an authentic bluesman. Elvis, Scotty and Bill started playing again, and this time

---

'If I could only find a white boy who could sing like a black man, I would make a lot of money.'
Sam Phillips to Marion Keisker

Phillips added echo, making the recording sound bigger and even more exciting.

The following night everyone returned to the studio and this time applied the opposite approach to their performance of bluegrass-godfather Bill Monroe's 'Blue Moon Of Kentucky'. At Bill Black's instigation they introduced a radical and urgent rhythm, playing the song in a more bluesy style than Monroe's original version. After several local disc jockeys had refused to programme it despite confirming that they enjoyed it – they felt that to play something so wild might jeopardize their jobs – Phillips contacted his unrelated namesake Dewey Phillips, whose 'Red Hot and Blue' programme regularly featured adventurous music that appealed to white teenagers who were not interested in the colour of a performer's skin. After playing the two tracks on station WHBQ in Memphis, Phillips was overwhelmed with telephone requests to hear them again. The Presley phenomenon was under way.

Phillips had recommended that, at least initially, Scotty Moore should act as Elvis's manager. Most of the income in those early days came from the trio's live shows, with Elvis calling himself the Hillbilly Cat, to emphasize his equal connections with coun-

LEFT: *The fusion of black and white musical styles gave Elvis's music the edge that producer Sam Phillips was looking for.*

try and rhythm-and-blues. Before long he was booked to appear on a major show headlined by famed country stars Slim Whitman and Marty Robbins. This was his first exposure to a big audience and it was a great success, although Elvis found their reaction to his uninhibited movements surprising. But if that show was a triumph, an appearance on Nashville's *Grand Ole Opry*, a live radio show, three months later, in September 1954, seemed disastrous. Because the trio sounded on record like a big group, everyone was surprised when

only three musicians arrived, and they were allowed to perform only the two tracks on their first single. Despite a cool reception from the *Opry's* rather conservative audience, the show led to a booking on a similar live radio show, the *Louisiana Hayride*, broadcast from Shreveport. After Elvis received an enthusiastic reaction, he was contracted to appear regularly on the show for a year.

A month after his first *Hayride* appearance, Elvis, who had continued to work for Crown Electric, gave up his day job, as did his colleagues. Drummer D.J. Fontana was hired to expand their sound, although Fontana did not play on their first single of 1955, 'Milkcow Blues Boogie'/'You're A Heartbreaker'. Soon after its release, Scotty Moore thankfully gave up managing the band, handing over the task to Bob Neal, a disc jockey who also ran a record shop in Memphis. Although Neal's arrival seemingly made little difference to Presley's music, the latter's first single after Neal's arrival, 'Baby Let's Play House'/'I'm Left, You're Right, She's Gone', became his first national (as opposed to local) hit, reaching the top five of the US country chart in the summer of 1955. This success attracted the attention of professional manager 'Colonel' Tom Parker (the rank was honorary), who

BELOW: *'Colonel' Tom Parker sensed enormous potential in the young Elvis.*

FACING PAGE: *Elvis rocks during a show in St Petersburg, Florida, 1956.*

already managed Eddy Arnold, an established country singer. Certainly, Parker's career before he began managing Elvis had been unorthodox. Before taking up artist management, he had made a living by running a stall in a circus, where one of his most famous attractions was 'Colonel Parker's Amazing Dancing Chickens'.

Parker had helped Neal with a live show by Elvis in New Mexico, and quickly developed a keen interest in the young singer when his name appeared in the hit parade. Parker sensed huge potential in this young rebel, and convinced Neal to relinquish his management deal, after which he launched his plan to make Presley the most famous name in popular music.

Parker took over just as the fifth Presley single, 'I Forget To Remember To Forget' (an archetypal country song title)/'Mystery Train' (a stunning version of an earlier Sun single by R & B star Little Junior Parker) was released. Parker saw his chance: if he could interest a big label in Elvis, everyone would make a lot of money. First he had to persuade Sam Phillips to relinquish his recording contract. With a Number One hit to his name, Phillips obviously wanted to keep Elvis if possible, but the deal Parker negotiated with RCA Records gave Phillips

$35,000 (an unheard-of sum for a new artist) in exchange for Elvis's Sun contract and all the recordings he had made for Sun (including a number that had not been released). The money tempted Phillips, who had also discovered four other young singers who later achieved worldwide fame – Johnny Cash, Jerry Lee Lewis, Roy Orbison and Carl Perkins – and he agreed to the offer. While he obviously might have

> *'When I first heard this boy, I detected a sensitivity and a talent that is boundless. This boy will go far.'*
>
> COLONEL PARKER

made $35 million if he had persevered with Presley, Phillips lacked the promotional resources RCA could muster.

In late 1955 Elvis Presley signed with RCA Records, for whom he would record for the rest of his life. His fame and fortune accelerated throughout 1956, as he accumulated dozens of hits and sold millions of records. Elvis travelled all over the United States during that first year as a rock-'n'-roll

RIGHT: *Elvis performs in Florida during a 1955 mini-tour.*

star, but returned to Memphis whenever he had a few days free of recording, promotion and concerts (which, inevitably, took up most of his time). On one of these visits home, in December 1956, he called in to Sun Studios where Jerry Lee Lewis and Johnny Cash were playing on a Carl Perkins recording session. Before long a jam session developed, as the four musicians sang mainly gospel songs for over an hour. Sam Phillips quickly realized that this was another historic event, and began recording it. A reporter who had been tipped off about what was happening remarked that this talented quartet could sell a million, and thereafter the four were known as the Million Dollar Quartet. Unfortunately for him, Sam Phillips was unable to release the recordings he made that day, since he had sold Elvis lock, stock and barrel to RCA only a year before. In fact, when the Million Dollar Quartet tracks were finally released in 1980, it was immediately obvious that they were of considerably greater historical than musical significance. Like many legendary records in the history of popular music, the whole amounted to considerably less than the sum of the parts.

KING OF ROCK 'N' ROLL

I've never been seriously hurt. I've had my hair pulled and a few scratches, and I've lost a few suits of clothes too, but as far as I'm concerned, if they want my shirt, they can have it. After all, they put it on my back to start with.'

If 1955 HAD seen Elvis Presley rise from obscurity to local fame in a short time with Sun, 1956 saw him ascend to the heights of international stardom with RCA. With Chet Atkins doubling as producer and second guitarist, Elvis went into RCA's Nashville studio with Scotty, Bill and D.J., and pianist Floyd Cramer. The two-day session, which took place just after Elvis's twenty-first birthday, produced five finished tracks. The most significant of these by far was 'Heartbreak Hotel', which gave Elvis his first pop chart hit, his first US Number One (which it remained for eight weeks!) and his first UK hit and top three single. Still widely regarded as one of the quintessential rock-'n'-roll records, the song was inspired by a news report of a suicide note – not the most cheerful subject.

Back on the road after the recording, the hysteria resulting from his live appearances often threatened Elvis with physical damage, although fortunately nothing untoward happened. The next milestone came at the end of January, when Elvis, Scotty, Bill and D.J. flew to New York for a nationally networked TV appearance on the *Jackie Gleason Stage Show*. The show's audience had been plummeting, and booking Elvis was seen as a potential life saver – executive pro-

FACING PAGE: *Elvis in 1956 with Natalie Wood, who was at one time tipped as a romantic interest.*

ducer Jack Philbin exclaimed, 'This kid is the guitar-playing Marlon Brando' and Philbin's assessment of Presley could not have been more accurate. His first major TV appearance provoked an unprecedented response: nothing like it had ever been seen on a family variety show, and there were as many complaints about his 'wiggling' as there were compliments. Even extremely

---

'It's impossible now to leave my hotel room. I remember one night I woke up starving, but I didn't dare go out for anything. I tried it once and the crowds were chasing me, and they smashed up an all-night delicatessen.'

---

prominent public figures were moved to comment, and great media weight was given to the likes of Billy Graham, who was quoted as saying, 'Elvis isn't the kind of boy I'd like my children to see'. Colonel Parker could hardly have wished for better publicity than the world-famous evangelist's insult, which enhanced Presley's standing as an anti-establishment icon.

FACING PAGE: *The cowboy movie* LOVE ME TENDER *was Elvis's big-screen debut.*

Soon after 'Heartbreak Hotel' had reached Number One, Hollywood, in the shape of noted film producer Hal Wallis, became interested. At the same time, with several more TV bookings from more prominent shows, Parker was soon able to increase the asking price for a live stage performance by Elvis to $10,000 a night and still find many takers. Elvis went to Hollywood at the start of March for a screen test, which he passed with flying colours, and was signed to a contract with Paramount for three films over the next seven years.

At the end of March Elvis's first LP was released, simply titled *Elvis Presley*. By the beginning of May it was at the top of the US LP chart, where it remained for ten weeks. It included several tracks inherited by RCA from Sam Phillips, as well as the Presley version of Carl Perkins's 'Blue Suede Shoes'. That song was released as the lead track of an EP also imaginatively titled 'Elvis Presley', which reached the Top Twenty of the US singles chart as the LP was zooming to the top. In July 'I Want You, I Need You, I Love You' topped the US singles list, and in August came the double-sided chart-topper, 'Don't Be Cruel' / 'Hound Dog' – three Number One singles in six months!

'Hound Dog', written by Leiber and Stoller in a quarter of an hour, was also a milestone because it was the first Presley track to feature The Jordanaires, the backing vocal quartet who would continue to work with Elvis for many years. The only negative aspect of the first half of the year was a debut season in Las Vegas, where audiences were older and more sophisticated and did not respond to the sight and sound that so

---

'It's affected my sleep, and I average about four or five hours a night. Everything has happened to me so fast in the last year and a half, I'm all mixed up – I can't keep up with everything that's happening.'

---

amazed their children. Any disappointment was soon forgotten when the Hillbilly Cat returned to Memphis, where he bought a $40,000 house for his parents.

Elvis's debut on the big screen was a cowboy movie originally titled *The Reno Brothers*, but renamed *Love Me Tender* when it

'Without Elvis, none of us could have made it.'
BUDDY HOLLY

became clear that the song of that title would be released as Elvis's new single. Advance orders for the new single topped 800,000, and the film was an inevitable box-office success following its premiere in New York in mid-November, although when Elvis 'died' in the movie, there was concern about how his fans might react. There was no need to worry. Elvis had become the new spearhead of rock 'n' roll, effortlessly elbowing Bill Haley from that position, and by his success encouraging the emergence of many other young rockers, including Gene Vincent, Little Richard, Chuck Berry, the Everly Brothers and

'I came along at a time in the music business when there was no trend. The people were looking for something different and I just came along in time.'

Buddy Holly. Elvis was modest about the role he played in others' success, and even about his own rise to fame. He could afford to be modest, as Colonel Parker took part of the credit: 'When I met him, he had a million dollar's worth of talent. Now, he has a million dollars.'

The first half of 1957 brought three more Number One singles, 'Too Much', 'All Shook Up' (also his first UK Number One) and 'Teddy Bear', which was the biggest hit from Elvis's second movie, *Loving You*. The film featured several songs performed as a band onstage, considerable consolation for its simplistic story-line, a continuing problem that would eventually damage Elvis's reputation beyond repair. That year also brought the acquisition of Graceland, the Memphis mansion that would remain Elvis's main residence for the rest of his life. Buying a big house was not a question of flaunting his fortune, but rather a way to provide some privacy for both himself and his long-suffering parents, whose house had been besieged by sightseers and souvenir hunters. Another imminent change was that the two musicians with whom he had found fame, Scotty Moore and Bill Black, decided to leave Elvis, principally because they felt their contribution to his

FACING PAGE: *Bill Haley was toppled as king of rock 'n' roll, handing the crown to Elvis.*

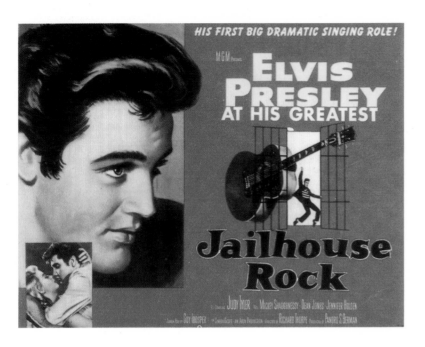

HIS FIRST BIG DRAMATIC SINGING ROLE!

MGM Presents
ELVIS
PRESLEY
AT HIS GREATEST

Jailhouse
Rock

Above: Jailhouse Rock demonstrated that Elvis could act as well as sing.

Facing page: Fans scream their approval at the world premiere of the film Loving You.

success merited more than the average $200 per week they were each paid. They appeared on screen in both *Loving You* and the follow-up, *Jailhouse Rock*. With the main songs by Leiber and Stoller, this was the best Presley movie to date, and augured well for the future, proving that Elvis was an acceptable actor as well as the most popular vocalist in the world.

The year had brought four more Number One singles, his third and fourth chart-topping LPs (*Loving You* and *Elvis's Christmas Album* – the latter considerably less

stomach-churning than might have been suspected), two more hugely successful films, a new home – and his draft notice. Elvis had been passed perfectly fit at a previous medical designed to establish his eligibility for military service and at the end of the year, received instructions that he was lucky enough to have been selected to train as a serviceman.

It may seem odd that the biggest pop star in the universe was unable to pull strings in high places that might have enabled him to avoid wearing fatigues and earning a pittance in place of the millions he could accumulate from films, records and concerts, but he was eventually persuaded to do what every other young American man was obliged to do at the time. Parker felt that it would pay immense dividends in terms of Elvis being more readily accepted by older generations. Even Elvis himself seemed convinced, telling a newspaper: 'I reckon I'll be able to handle the Army assignment OK. I'll do whatever they tell me, and I won't be asking for special favours.' In many ways, he was as good as his word – although his US army contemporaries might have disagreed with his last assertion as, ultimately, Elvis was allowed to live in a rented house with his friends and family.

G.I. IN GERMANY

'It's a duty I've got to fill, and I'm gonna do it. I guess the only thing I'll hate about it is leaving my mama. She's always been my best girl.'

On becoming a G.I.

ALTHOUGH ELVIS had declared himself ready to serve his country, Paramount Pictures were less than impressed to learn that the rising star in whose career they had invested a lot of money (and received a good deal more in return) was going to be unavailable to proceed with his fourth film, *King Creole*, unless his term in uniform could be delayed. Paramount pressured Elvis to ask for a postponement of the original starting date of his military service, and a three month extension was granted, provoking complaints from others whose applications for a delay had been refused. However, it was clear that Elvis was not trying to avoid his obligations. During the early part of 1958 he travelled by train to Hollywood from Memphis, a much more time-consuming journey than a flight, but one almost certainly planned by Colonel Parker to make Elvis very visible to his many fans, who congregated at each station along the route hoping to catch a brief glimpse of their idol.

King Creole was a rather more ambitious movie than its predecessors. It was based to some extent on *A Stone For Danny Fisher*, a novel by Harold Robbins. Overall, the critical reaction to the film was positive, a fairly rare occurrence as very few Presley movies

had any redeeming features. Before it was released in the middle of the year, there had been the customary succession of new single releases, starting with 'Don't', another composition by Leiber and Stoller, which became Presley's tenth Number One single in less than two years. The follow-up, 'Wear My Ring Around Your Neck', did not take the pole position in the US singles chart.

By then Elvis was in a US Army training camp, where he learned the basics of army life as Private US53310761. Elvis was stationed at Fort Hood in Texas for two

'My induction notice says for me to leave my car at home, as transportation will be provided. They tell me just to bring a razor, a toothbrush, a comb and enough money to last two weeks.'

months, after which he was allowed two weeks' leave, which he spent in Memphis, apart from two days in RCA's Nashville studio, where he cut five new tracks. This would be the only recording session he undertook during his period as a GI, which

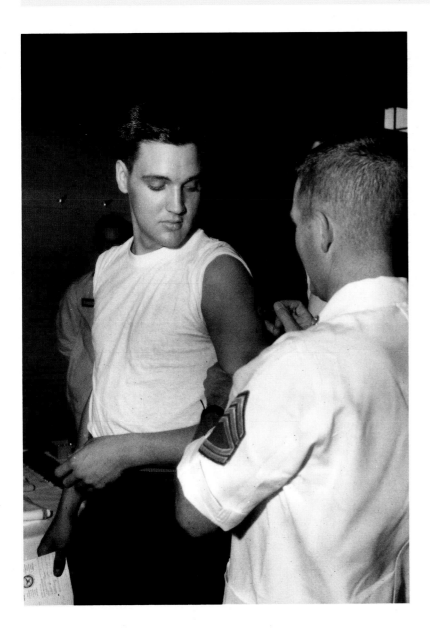

gave RCA and Colonel Parker the problem of how to maintain his following for the next year and a half.

There was already one potential hit single included among the *King Creole* songs, 'Hard Headed Woman' (which restored him to Number One in July), but after that, it would have to be one of the tracks recorded during that session in June, which was his last during the 1950s. On the album front, fans were kept happy by the release of *Elvis's Golden Records*, a lavishly packaged collection of all his biggest hits up to and including 'Jailhouse Rock', which became his first platinum (million-selling) album, and was followed later in the year by the *King Creole* soundtrack album, which also reached the US top three. Fortunately, there were some classics among the newly recorded tracks, which were Presley's first studio (as opposed to film soundtrack) sessions undertaken without Scotty Moore and Bill Black — while Moore would return to the fray during the 1960s, Bill Black never again worked with Elvis. The final 1958 single by Elvis featured one of the new tracks, the frantic 'I Got Stung', backed with his cover version of a 1956 hit by New Orleans bluesman Smiley Lewis, 'One Night Of Sin'. After Elvis recorded this song with the original

LEFT: *'Army shoots Presley', said the headlines — Elvis takes his injections like a man.*

ABOVE: *On his first leave from the army, Elvis escorted his parents to a premiere of his new film,* KING CREOLE.

lyrics, it was decided to tone it down and it was re-recorded as simply 'One Night'. Both sides of the single reached the US Top Ten, only his third single to achieve this considerable feat, following 'Don't Be Cruel'/'Hound Dog' and 'Don't'/'I Beg Of You'.

During that summer Vernon and Gladys had temporarily moved to Texas to be near their son, particularly because Gladys had become quite ill and Elvis was extremely concerned about her health. Sadly, it continued to worsen, to the point where it was

decided that she must return to Memphis to be near her own doctor. Soon after her return to Graceland, she was moved into a local hospital, and Elvis was allowed compassionate leave to visit her. However, her condition proved incurable and on 14 August 1958 she died of a heart attack. Elvis was devastated: 'I was the only child, and Mama was always right with me.'

A month later Elvis was posted to Germany, travelling by sea on his first (and only) trip to Europe. Never missing a trick and probably at the behest of Colonel Parker, RCA recorded the press conference Elvis gave just before the USS *General Randall* cast off. The recording would be released as an EP titled 'Elvis Sails' in early 1959, but as it contained no music, merely Elvis answering questions from newsmen, it failed to trouble the chart compilers. However, it was totally overshadowed by a genuine new single, both sides of which again made the US Top Ten independently. 'A Fool Such As I' was an energetic cover version of a 1953 country hit by Hank Snow, while 'I Need Your Love Tonight' was a no-holds-barred rock 'n' roll original, and both had been recorded during that two day session when Elvis was on leave in Memphis before his Texas posting.

LEFT: *Elvis's military service was delayed until the completion of filming for KING CREOLE.*

The press conference revealed little of note beyond the news that Elvis was looking forward to a European tour after his discharge. Sadly, this never occurred. Later, it was strongly rumoured that Colonel Parker had always found excuses for postponing a European tour because he was concerned that if he (Parker) left the United States, he might not be allowed to return. It seems that Parker's anxiety was caused by the fact

LEFT: *The world's most eligible bachelor, Elvis's name was linked with that of many of his leading ladies.*

'I'd probably starve to death if rock 'n' roll died! If it ever did happen, and I don't think it would, I'd make a serious try to keep on top in movies.'

that he was an illegal immigrant, a Dutchman named Andreas van Kuijk, who had entered the United States in the late 1920s without a passport.

The other major revelation of the press conference was that Vernon Presley and Elvis's grandmother would be relocating to Germany to be near their pride and joy. If Parker was indeed an illegal immigrant, he would not wish to move to Germany, and Vernon's proximity to Elvis would prevent

'One of the last things Mom said was that Daddy and I should always be together, so wherever they send me, Daddy will go too.'

the latter from insisting on Parker's presence.

During his time in Germany Elvis met Priscilla Beaulieu, the fourteen-year-old daughter of a US Air Force major. Despite their age difference – Elvis was then twenty-

'Priscilla is very mature, very intelligent and the most beautiful girl I've ever seen, but there's no romance, it's nothing serious.'

four, and the most eligible bachelor in the world – he was particularly impressed that she was so unimpressed by his fame. They were to marry seven years later.

There was one final new unreleased track, 'A Big Hunk O' Love', which would be Elvis's last single for nine months and therefore needed to be a monster hit. It was, becoming his only Number One single of 1959. Two compilation albums seemed to stop the fans becoming restive: *A Date With Elvis*, a thrown-together album including five of the early Sun recordings and tracks from the film soundtracks, is regarded as being one of his finest LPs, although it was outsold by *For LP Fans Only*, which con-

tained a similar hotchpotch. The end of 1959 brought *Elvis's Gold Records Volume 2 – 50,000,000 Elvis Fans Can't Be Wrong*, whose sleeve featured Elvis wearing a gold lamé suit designed by a Hollywood showbiz tailor. With his discharge now within sight, Elvis had survived his national service, but it would become clear as the 1960s progressed that he had apparently forgotten how to rock.

ABOVE: *The epitome of US manhood: Elvis at the wheel with a broad-brimmed hat and a fistful of dollars.*

HOLLYWOOD

'I had a letter recently suggesting that I should get drunk or something in my movies, but the type I'm making now are doing so well that it would be silly to change the formula — I've done eleven films and they've all made money. A certain type of audience likes me and it would be foolish to tamper with that kind of success.'

FACING PAGE: *Viva Las Vegas (1964) with leading lady, Ann-Margret, one of the many celebrities who starred alongside Elvis.*

HAVING SUCCESSFULLY negotiated Elvis's military service without losing much momentum, it was a relieved Colonel Parker who tackled the problem of celebrating the star's return with the biggest possible impact. Television offered the greatest audience potential, and Frank Sinatra was due to host a TV special. Even though Sinatra, in a famous quote, had called rock 'n' roll 'phoney and false, sung, written and played by cretinous goons', the previous TV Special bearing his name had attracted too small an audience for comfort, and he needed a big star to ensure that this one avoided a similar fate. There was only one name in the frame, so Parker asked (and received) $125,000 for Elvis to appear.

The show was recorded in late March 1960. As well as performing both sides of his first post-army single, 'Stuck On You'/'Fame and Fortune' (which he had recorded a few days before), he also sang two duets with 'Ol' Blue Eyes': one of the latter's hits, 'Witchcraft', and one of his own, 'Love Me Tender'. Other guests on the show included Sammy Davis Jr and Sinatra's daughter Nancy: eight years later, she would co-star in one of Elvis's latter-day movies, *Speedway*. In fact, Elvis spent most of those eight years starring in rotten feature films, neglecting his talent as a vocalist. It was hard to fault Parker's philosophy on this score, as Elvis's movies would be seen by far more fans all over the world than would have the chance to see him onstage, and their release would also help to promote his new records, some of which would be featured in the films. Parker's misjudgement was in his desire to make Presley a so-

---

'I'm gonna let my sideburns grow a little, but I doubt if they'll be as long as they were; I've got over that kick, I'll just consider doing what comes naturally.'

---

called 'family entertainer', who would appeal to an audience from seven to seventy. Before the advent of rock 'n' roll, this was a laudable aim, but record-buyers were no longer mainly from the middle-aged establishment. They now included a fast-growing number of younger people, who regarded the values of their parents as old-fashioned and highly suspect.

The first priority for Elvis after the TV special was to record some new material, and 'Stuck On You', released within a month of his return, quickly topped the US chart. The same session found him starting work on a new LP, *Elvis Is Back!*, which became a big seller. Unfortunately, it would be Elvis's last original album of any significance for eight years, until he finally escaped from the soundtrack treadmill, which was the result of Parker's misplaced strategy of cinematic concentration.

Another Number One single followed, 'It's Now Or Never', based on a vintage Italian ballad, 'O Sole Mio'. The end of 1960 brought the first of the terrible movies, *GI Blues*, which was conceived to

---

'I don't consider the new crop of singers as rivals; I've always believed there's room in show business for everyone.'

---

remind its audience that Elvis had been in the US Army, and featured footage shot in Germany (although care was taken not to film the star while he was still on active service, to avoid potential criticism). The soundtrack included few highlights, but was

still an improvement on a pathetic plot, which featured Elvis singing to a doll. It is to the eternal credit of RCA that they decided not to release the song involved,

---

'I don't know about marriage. I guess I'll wait until the bug bites, and it hasn't yet.'

'Wooden Heart', as a single in the United States. In Britain, however, bad taste prevailed and 'Wooden Heart' became Presley's seventh Number One single, after the only slightly superior 'Are You Lonesome Tonight', which was released at the end of the year and included a rather sickly monologue.

Early 1961 brought a second transatlantic Number One with Italian roots, 'Surrender', based on 'Come Back to Sorrento'. It coincided with another decidedly forgettable movie, *Flaming Star*, an unimpressive Western in which Elvis hardly sang, thus removing what little point there was in the film.

Colonel Parker decided that, in future, every Elvis film must include more songs. He established a routine whereby each year

'We shot Kissin' Cousins in seventeen days, and I think that was the turning point in Presley films. Up until then, certain standards were maintained, but that was when we noticed that there was no rehearsal for all the numbers.'

LANCE LEGAULT, WHO APPEARED IN SEVERAL ELVIS FILMS

RIGHT: *In films such as* BLUE HAWAII, *Elvis maintained his fame — if not his reputation as an actor.*

would bring three new films, four new singles and three new LPs, although the LPs nearly always turned out to be soundtrack albums. Occasional singles were the only redeeming feature of this period, like the late 1961 double A-side, 'Little Sister' / 'His Latest Flame', the same year's dramatic ballad, 'Can't Help Falling In Love' (from the movie *Blue Hawaii*, whose soundtrack LP undeservedly topped the album charts on both sides of the Atlantic); and three reasonable 45s from 1962, 'Good Luck Charm', 'She's Not You' and 'Return To Sender'.

Little purpose would be served by listing the titles of the Presley feature films

'It was getting harder and harder singing to the camera all day long. Let's face it, when you have ten different songs for each movie, they can't all be good. Eventually, I got tired of singing to turtles and guys I'd just beaten up.'

RIGHT: *GIRLS! GIRLS! GIRLS!* (1962) was one of less memorable films Elvis made in the 1960s.

made between 1962 and 1968, although some of the screen celebrities with whom he appeared – Charles Bronson and Gig Young in *Kid Galahad* (1962); Ursula Andress in *Fun In Acapulco* (1963); Ann-Margret in *Viva Las Vegas* (1964), whose title song was superior to the vast majority of second-rate soundtrack material from his movies; Barbara Stanwyck in *Roustabout* (1964); Nancy Sinatra in the previously mentioned *Speedway* (1968); Mary Tyler Moore in *Change Of Habit* (1970), thankfully his final dumb film of the era – suggested that appearing in a Presley movie must be well paid, as it was unlikely to enhance any-one's cinematic career. The only halfway reasonable albums from this time were two gospel collections, *His Hand In Mine* (1961) and *How Great Thou Art*.

ABOVE: *Nancy Sinatra starred alongside Elvis in SPEEDWAY (1968).*

1953 R-&-B classic by the Orioles) was actually recorded during the sessions for *His Hand In Mine*, but had been omitted from that album. There was nothing else of much value to the uncommitted until 1967/8, when three consecutive singles, 'Big Boss Man', 'Guitar Man' and 'US Male' reawakened interest, before one of the worst films, *Stay Away, Joe* made it clear that this must have been an aberration. In August 1965, Elvis met The Beatles at his house in Bel Air.

It was an appalling artistic decline in quality from the merely poor to the downright dreadful, but, regrettably, many of the movies made a profit. Even the singles only occasionally failed to disappoint: 1963's 'Devil In Disguise' was adequate, as was 1964's 'Ain't That Loving You Baby', which, although it wasn't a big hit, sounded like the Elvis of the 1950s (hardly surprising, as it had been recorded in 1958), while 1965's 'Crying in the Chapel' (a cover of a

BELOW: *Graceland was Elvis's sanctuary from the glare of publicity.*

LEFT: *In the midst of a horde of fans, Priscilla Beaulieu waves goodbye to Elvis.*

RIGHT: *In 1967, Elvis Presley married Priscilla Beaulieu in Las Vegas.*

'I prefer to think of them as members of a little country club I run. Most of them are my friends from back home, they're not bodyguards. One is my accountant, another my travel consultant. I need a valet, a security officer and a wardrobe man with me nearly all the time.'

ON THE MEMBERS OF THE

SO-CALLED MEMPHIS MAFIA

John Lennon noted at the time, 'There was only one person in the United States that we really wanted to meet.'

The only real highlight of this barren period was that Elvis got married in 1967 to Priscilla Beaulieu, the young girl he had met in Germany, and who was now twenty-one years old. She had been living at Graceland since 1962, and it is felt that she and Elvis would have been married some time before had Colonel Parker not advised against it, on the basis that it might detract from the appeal of the films if their star was known to be married. Elvis's patience was eventually exhausted. The marriage took place in Las Vegas at around 3 am on 1 May, 1967, with less than a dozen guests in attendance, among them two of Elvis's large constant entourage, known to the media as the 'Memphis Mafia' – a description Elvis disliked intensely. Unfortunately, there was negative publicity about unnecessarily violent behaviour towards fans by some of these hangers-on, which they justified by the need to protect Elvis from danger. Little did anyone realise that by their refusal to disagree with Elvis on any topic at all, these 'companions' were arguably the greatest danger he ever faced.

'We decided to get married about six months ago. Priscilla was one of the few girls who was interested in me for me alone. We never discussed marriage in Germany, we just met at her father's house, went to the movies and did a lot of driving, that's all. I waited for her to grow up.'

LAS VEGAS

'You can't go on doing the same thing year after year. It's been a long time since I've done anything professionally except make movies and cut albums. Before too long, I'm going to make some personal appearances, because I miss the personal contact with audiences.'

It MAY HAVE BEEN because he was married and now felt much more responsible than in his carefree bachelor days that Elvis belatedly came to the same conclusion that had been arrived at by innumerable lapsed fans during the dreadful mid-Sixties: he had to perform in public again. There was another possible reason for this new

---

'Elvis, I got to talk to you, you got to listen this one time. Son, you're spending money faster than we're making it.'

VERNON PRESLEY

---

approach: despite the continuing popularity of his ghastly movies and occasional big-hit records, Elvis was spending money faster than he could earn it. After paying $30,000 to buy a ranch at Walls, a tiny town very near the Mississippi-Tennessee state line, Elvis then spent over $250,000 equipping it with mobile homes for his entourage, a high-security fence and a fleet of trucks. He had also purchased a $400,000 Beverly Hills mansion less than a

week after his wedding, along with a stable of prize-winning horses. In addition to this expenditure he was employing nearly two dozen people.

Vernon was eventually so concerned about the situation that he confided in Colonel Parker, who was propelled into action by the realization that his golden goose was seemingly egg-bound. Parker opted for a TV Special, sponsored by Singer Sewing Machines. Elvis was to be paid half a million dollars for playing two live dates at NBC's television studios in Burbank, Los Angeles. Singer would be given exclusive rights to sell an Elvis LP, a patchy compilation of soundtrack material, in their stores — perhaps it was used as a giveaway with each substantial purchase.

Before all this happened, Elvis became a father on 1 February 1968, nine months to the day after his nuptials. Although Elvis was

---

'Oh man, she's just great! I'm still a little shaky! She's a doll, she's great — I felt all along she'd be a girl.'

ON THE BIRTH OF HIS DAUGHTER

Left: *Elvis and Priscilla prepare to leave hospital with their new daughter, Lisa-Marie.*

the subject of many paternity suits, Lisa Marie was the King's only acknowledged offspring.

Perhaps inspired by fatherhood, Elvis gave an immaculate performance in the hour-long TV Special, which was recorded in June 1968, and screened that Christmas, and featured a sequence where he was backed by a small group that included Scotty Moore and D.J. Fontana. Even if the entire show wasn't wall-to-wall wonderful, enough was sufficiently superb to bring back a number of disenchanted fans, and the resulting *Elvis – NBC-TV Special* LP (his first official live album) was his first to reach the US Top Ten in three years. It was felt by many commentators that the major reason for the TV Special's success in artistic terms was that Parker wasn't calling the shots. Steve Binder, who directed the show, supposedly won Elvis's confidence by telling him that while he may have been one of the world's greatest celebrities, he would be able to walk in the streets of Hollywood without causing a riot. Elvis, having been used to hysteria wherever he went for over ten years, scoffed, until Binder told him to walk along Sunset Boulevard: Elvis was surprised to find that Binder had been absolutely correct. Sightings of celebrities on Sunset

RIGHT: *It was said that Elvis's stage movements 'must have made Jim Morrison green with envy'.*

Strip, if not an everyday occurrence, were certainly not infrequent, while another item of relevance was that in 1968 the Strip was the hippest place on earth, and at this point Elvis was a laughing stock in comparison with Jim Morrison, Jimi Hendrix and other hippie heroes. The TV special was a smash hit, and media praise came from both the establishment and the underground; *Eye* magazine suggested that Elvis's body movements 'must have made Jim Morrison green with envy'.

'There are several unbelievable things about Elvis, but the most incredible is his staying power in a world where meteoric careers fade like shooting stars.'

NEWSWEEK

It was, of course, impossible for Elvis to escape from his outstanding movie commitments, and there were four more turkeys to be made before that depressing phase was finally laid to rest. The redeeming feature of 1969 was that Elvis undertook some recording sessions in Memphis rather than Nashville, working with local session musicians and a new producer, 'Chips' Moman. The first hit from the Memphis sessions was 'In The Ghetto', his first Top 3 single since 1965, then came another gold album (a rarity in the previous five years) *From Elvis In Memphis*. Next was 'Suspicious Minds', a well-deserved Number One single and his first US chart-topper since 'Good Luck Charm' in 1962, followed at the end of 1969 by 'Don't Cry Daddy', a third US Top Ten single in six months.

Another gold album came at the end of the year too, but its power was somewhat diluted because it was a double LP, the first half titled *From Memphis To Vegas* (containing tracks recorded live at the International Hotel, Las Vegas, in August that year), and the second *From Vegas To Memphis* (with more muscular tracks from the sessions in Memphis earlier in the year). Colonel Parker decided that the next thing was to get Elvis back onstage. The obvious place for this was Las Vegas, where America's most opulent people holidayed and were entertained by the world's greatest stars. Las Vegas had several other advantages – performers were booked for a season, obviating the need to travel, and the fees they

were paid were astronomical. Of course, Parker negotiated tigerishly for the best deal, and Elvis was booked for a season at the Hilton. Despite a generally disappointing decade in the Sixties, Elvis was still a major attraction.

As he did not wish to return to the frantic style of his pre-army days, Elvis assembled a backing band for his return to live work. Elvis and his new band debuted at the end of July 1969, and the huge success of the month-long season led to a repeat booking in early 1970, which also produced a live LP, although this time largely comprising new material of good quality, including Tony Joe White's 'Polk Salad Annie', the Creedence Clearwater Revival hit, 'Proud Mary', and Joe South's 'Walk A Mile In My Shoes'. Titled *On Stage – February 1970*, this was another gold LP, as was his sixth chart album of the year, *Elvis – That's The Way It Is*. This was the soundtrack to a TV documentary filmed during the build-up to a third Las Vegas season and also incorporated highlights from his onstage performances. Colonel Parker was obviously back in control of the situation – whenever anyone staying at the Hilton Hotel ordered anything from room service, they also received a catalogue with details of Elvis records current-

LEFT: *Colonel Parker was a fierce protector of Elvis's material interests.*

LEFT: *Priscilla was not permitted to travel with Elvis when he was on tour, so the couple saw little of each other*

'My first meeting with Colonel Parker was five hours after Mr. Hilton took over the hotel. I came in at noon and had a meeting with Colonel Parker at five. Tom Jones, Engelbert Humperdinck and Barbra Streisand are all great stars, but there is only one who sells out the entire duration of an engagement as soon as his name is announced.'

THE VICE-PRESIDENT OF THE HILTON HOTEL, LAS VEGAS

LEFT: *Fans in Europe were disappointed that Elvis never toured overseas.*

ly available. By the time the season started, that catalogue included another US Top Ten single, 'The Wonder Of You' (the thirty-seventh by Presley to reach these heights). Parker seemed to have retrieved a situation that had shown signs of going rapidly down-hill, but Elvis's return to live performance also produced an immediate demand from the world outside North America to see him onstage, particularly in Europe. The same problems as before concerned the Colonel and rather than risk being treated as

an illegal alien, Parker developed a strategy to discourage overseas tours by demanding ludicrously large sums (reportedly millions of dollars) before he would even consider the possibility – as he told one European promoter, 'That'll be fine for me, but how much are you gonna pay my boy?' This was ultimately the major reason why Presley's millions of European fans were never able to see their hero onstage.

LEFT: *Performing 'Jailhouse Rock' (always a crowd-pleaser) on stage.*

CRITICAL DECLINE

'Maybe it's time for Elvis to retire. At forty,
his records are increasingly uneven, his choice
of material sometimes ludicrous and his concert
performances often sloppy. Worst of all,
there is no purpose or personal vision in
his music anymore.'

LOS ANGELES TIMES, 1975

FACING PAGE: *A rare shot of the happy family —
Elvis and Priscilla with daughter Lisa-Marie.*

ARGUABLY, 1970 had been Elvis's best year for nearly a decade, but the return to live performance had its down side, ultimately inflating the one-time hunk into an overweight pill freak. The pressure of performing late at night and sleeping only during the day resulted in an unnatural

---

'I saw a woman run down the aisle at full speed and launch herself like an Evel Knievel motorcycle. From four rows back, she took a leap, sailed through the air and landed with a splat, skidding across the stage. Elvis saw her coming and side-stepped her and she slid right into the drums.'

FILM-MAKER BOB ABEL ON ELVIS'S SHOW IN LAS VEGAS IN 1971

---

life, which necessitated the taking of sleeping pills. As Jerry Schilling, one of Presley's associates, noted 'We lived long hours, slept in the daytime and took pills to make it easier.' When an early start was called

for, so were amphetamines for instant energy; this led to addiction, which produced physical and mental deterioration. While Elvis was enjoying a renaissance in musical terms, it was at a terrible cost. No one could have suspected the grim outcome when the first 1971 LP, *Elvis Country ('I'm 10,000 Years Old')* was widely praised. In musical terms the rest of that year was a total washout, hardly helped by a totally uncritical, largely female fan-following for the two seasons of Las Vegas shows, each lasting a month.

If the fans remained delirious that their hero was more available than in the previous decade, the critics were more objective. For example, as early as 1971 the *Hollywood Reporter* observed: 'Elvis Presley's show at the Las Vegas Hilton is sloppy, hurriedly rehearsed, uneven, mundanely lit, poorly amplified, occasionally monotonous, often silly and haphazardly co-ordinated.' The over-protective insulation of the Memphis Mafia almost certainly suppressed such honest and accurate views, no doubt fearing that bringers of bad tidings might find themselves out of work as a result, because their employer was constantly under the influence of a pharmaceutical cocktail that made him irrational.

LEFT: *After six years of marriage, Elvis and Priscilla were divorced in 1973.*

The next year, 1972, was notable chiefly for the fact that Priscilla, finally bored by his unspouse-like behaviour, left Elvis. He was rarely at home, partly due to his performing commitments and partly due to his hell-raising with his 'friends' on the payroll. Priscilla was not permitted to travel with Elvis when he was on tour – in the early 1970s, he undertook a handful of live dates between

'We are the best of friends and always have been. Our divorce came about not because of another man, but because of circumstances involving my career, nothing else, regardless of what you have read or have been led to believe. I don't think it was fair on Priscilla, with me gone so often and travelling so much.'

Vegas seasons, from which Priscilla was also barred after opening nights. She eventually fell in love with her karate teacher, Mike Stone, who ran a martial-arts school in California. Elvis was mortified: it had never occurred to him that his wife might leave

him, but in February 1972 he and Priscilla were legally separated, and divorce proceedings began six months later.

Elvis's next significant professional engagement was a tour of the southern United States, which was to be filmed for a documentary imaginatively titled *Elvis On Tour*, produced and directed by the same movie makers who had been responsible for the acclaimed *Mad Dogs and Englishmen*, the story of a tour by Joe Cocker in 1970. The film also included footage from the classic TV shows screened before Elvis went into the army, and (perhaps to balance such glories) moments from some of the awful Sixties movies. For a change, there was no soundtrack album, but the film did introduce fans outside the United States to the use of 'Also Sprach Zarathustra' (as memorably used in the film *2001 – A Space Odyssey*) to herald Elvis's arrival onstage. The film crew could hardly believe the commotion that resulted each night: flash bulbs exploding, women screaming, general pandemonium. The lack of a live album didn't faze Parker: he simply arranged to record another concert, during a three-night stand at Madison Square Garden in New York. This time critics praised Elvis, the writer from *Variety* calling him 'a highly polished,

FACING PAGE: *Elvis holds a press conference at the New York Hilton in 1972.*

perfectly timed, spectacularly successful show business machine'.

From having started so disastrously on a personal level for Elvis, the year was relatively upbeat professionally, with a few good singles. His version of Mickey Newbury's 'An American Trilogy' wasn't a big hit but it became a staple of his live show, while 'Burning Love', a stunning song by country writer Dennis Linde, was Elvis's final US

BELOW: *ELVIS ON TOUR immortalized the performer's tour of the southern United States.*

top three hit during his lifetime. On the flip-side of his next US single, 'Separate Ways' (from the *Elvis On Tour* film), was a song that later became a standard of the 1980s, 'Always On My Mind'. Released as a single in Britain for Christmas 1972, it was a Top Ten hit, but Elvis's version has never reached the US chart. *Elvis As Recorded At Madison Square Garden* went platinum, an increasingly rare occurrence for a Presley album, and the project was a major success. *Aloha from Hawaii via Satellite* was also a huge success, spawning yet another live album, his sixth since 1968, but one that restored Elvis to the top of the US album chart for the first time since 1964. In 1973 Elvis produced only two hit singles, less than any year since 1956.

Already paranoid, Elvis had acquired a tame physician known as 'Dr Nick', who could be prevailed upon to supply whatever the world-famous hypochondriac decided he needed. After his divorce was finalized in October 1973, Elvis slipped rapidly downhill. While she was still in regular contact with him, Priscilla had nagged Elvis about his drug-taking, his lifestyle and his general condition, but after she was no longer around to make him occasionally feel guilty, Elvis did exactly as he pleased. None of the

ABOVE: *Tom Jones and Elvis Presley shared many qualities in their on-stage performances.*

albums. *Having Fun With Elvis On Stage* provoked a Presley biographer to write: 'If God had wanted Elvis to be a professional comedian, he would have given him a funny nose, baggy pants, a banana skin and an exploding guitar.' The only bright spot of a poor year was a cover version of Chuck Berry's 'Promised Land' released as a single, which reached the UK Top Ten. It is interesting to note that while only two singles by Presley had reached the US Top Ten during the 1970s, this was his fourteenth to reach those heights in the UK chart; perhaps because he never performed outside the United States, the rest of the world still regarded him with awe. It was true again in 1975, a vintage year in Britain for Presley LPs, although *40 Greatest Hits* (which topped the UK chart) and *The Sun Collection* (widely regarded as the greatest Presley compilation ever released) contained nothing new. Neither would have been conceived had Colonel Parker still been

Memphis Mafia dared contradict their employer and friend. Some of them subsequently maintained that they would do whatever he asked because they viewed him as virtually omniscient.

1974 was a woeful year. It included another moderately successful live album, this time recorded in Memphis, but also the very worst Elvis LP ever, one containing no music, but spoken introductions and between-songs talk from the numerous live

'Well, no one ever asks Elvis to play for free.'
COLONEL PARKER, ON BEING TOLD NO ONE GETS PAID TO PLAY FOR PRESIDENT NIXON

'You can't have that Cadillac, it's mine, but never mind, I'll buy you another. Go into the showroom and pick the one you like.'

TO A FAN WHO ADMIRED HIS CAR

'Since his return to live performing, Elvis has apparently lost interest. He's not just a little out of shape, not just a bit chubbier than usual, the living legend is fat and ludicrously aping his former self.'

HOLLYWOOD REPORTER

in control of the Presley catalogue, but in 1973, he had sold this treasure trove to RCA Records for a reputed $5.5 million, apparently not only because Elvis was still spending money like a drunken sailor, but because Parker himself had suffered a long losing streak on the Las Vegas gambling tables.

'The lips of the trumpet players were so cold they could barely blow their horns, and the strings on our guitars kept changing key. We were glad to get out of there.'
JOHN WILKINSON, ON PLAYING OUTDOORS IN DETROIT ON NEW YEAR'S EVE, 1975

FACING PAGE AND RIGHT: US President Nixon invited Elvis to perform at the White House (one of the greatest accolades for any entertainer); however, Parker was adamant that Elvis must receive a fee for his services, so the event never occurred.

The critics also began to sharpen their knives again, and their criticism was entirely justified. The entire strategy that had kept Elvis in a prominent position in the music industry seemed to have been abandoned. One extreme example was the decision to play an outdoor concert in Detroit on New Year's Eve 1975, when it was bitterly cold. Elvis had lost the plot completely.

DEATH AND AFTERMATH

'The thing that was most difficult to accept and
probably the primary reason that I ultimately left
was that there was no room for personal growth.
Your life revolved entirely around Elvis.'
LINDA THOMPSON ON WHY SHE LEFT ELVIS

FACING PAGE: *According to witnesses, Elvis had to be restrained from
destroying loudspeakers with a shotgun while recording in 1976.*

THE NEW YEAR, 1976, was even more of a washout than the one just past. Elvis grew fatter, which led to a lengthy catalogue of medical problems, including swollen legs, an enlarged heart and various other results of obesity. This, in turn, led to several members of the Memphis Mafia experiencing marital problems, as they were obliged to spend long hours at Graceland with their ailing boss. Even Elvis's girlfriend of four years, Linda Thompson, abandoned him. Of course, there was someone else to take her place, Ginger Alden, who remained with Elvis for the rest of his life. Things became so bad that RCA Records, realizing that they were unlikely to convince Elvis to return to either their Nashville or Los Angeles studio, took recording equipment to Graceland in February 1976. The results were adequate, if predictably nothing to write home about, and From Elvis Presley Boulevard, Memphis, Tennessee didn't reach the top forty of the US album chart. Only two singles were released in the United States in 1976. The second of the pair, 'Moody Blue', reached the UK Top Ten in 1977, and it became the title track of the final LP released during Elvis Presley's lifetime.

LEFT: *Elvis's increasing weight led to a range of medical problems, and hampered his strenuous live performances.*

RIGHT: *Some people felt that Elvis: What Happened? was written as an act of revenge by Elvis's ex-employees.*

Its release almost coincided with the publication of the book, *Elvis: What Happened?*, written by three former members of the Memphis Mafia, Red West, his brother Sonny, and Dave Hebler, with journalist Steve Dunleavy. The trio had been fired by Vernon Presley on the basis that they were too vigorous towards members of the public. Red and Sonny West, who had been friendly with Elvis since they were at school together, were particularly mortified, and their book revealed many aspects of Elvis's post-divorce self-indulgence, providing seemingly credible information on his excessive drug use and other details of his hedonistic lifestyle. An advance copy was sent to Graceland shortly before it was published, and it is interesting

'He will read it and he will be hopping mad at us because he will know that every word is the truth, but maybe, just maybe, it will do him some good.'
SONNY WEST ON HOW HE THOUGHT ELVIS WOULD REACT TO READING HIS BOOK

to note that while it is acknowledged that Elvis had read parts of it (and was most displeased with what he regarded as betrayal by lifelong friends), any attempts made to suppress its publication were unsuccessful.

After a concert in Indianapolis on 26 June, Elvis returned to Graceland. He intended to spend time with Ginger Alden and perhaps more importantly from his point of view, with Lisa-Marie, who was then eight years old, and was scheduled to spend a longer time away from her mother and exclusively in her father's care than ever before. Elvis went to bed at 6 am on 16 August, taking eight sleeping pills of varying types. Still unable to sleep, he made

'Elvis had the arteries of an eighty-year-old man. His body was just worn out, and his arteries and veins were terribly corroded.' A HOSPITAL SPOKESMAN

'Elvis Presley's death deprives our country of a part of itself. He was both unique and irreplaceable.' PRESIDENT JIMMY CARTER

'Whenever Elvis was admitted to the hospital, there were always rumours that he was dead, so I took it with a grain of salt. Elvis was nude and his head was over the edge of the table, and my first impression was that he was dead. His head was blue.' A SPOKESMAN AT THE MEMPHIS BAPTIST MEMORIAL HOSPITAL

a telephone call to 'Dr Nick's' office and asked a nurse for more medication; the nurse was probably the last person to have a conversation with Elvis. At two o'clock that afternoon, Ginger woke up and found herself alone in bed. Elvis did not reply to her calls, and she found him face down on the bathroom floor. She raised the alarm immediately, and Elvis was rushed to the Memphis Baptist Memorial Hospital, where he was pronounced dead. The news

RIGHT: *20,000 mourners filed past Elvis's coffin in Graceland.*

was suppressed until Vernon Presley could be informed; it then quickly spread around the world.

The coroner held a press conference, where he told the world that Elvis had died of cardiac arrhythmia, a heart attack, stressing that this was a natural death and that the body showed no evidence of drug abuse. This was the ultimate cover-up.

The reaction of the general public was remarkable. Thousands of people kept a vigil outside the gates of Graceland, and it seemed as though this death had provoked as much grief among the American people as the assassination of President John Kennedy in 1963. In Britain, where death often signals an astonishing increase in record sales, RCA were quick off the mark in making sure that shops were full of Elvis singles and albums, and in the last four months of 1977, fourteen Presley singles (mainly re-issues such as 'All Shook Up', 'Return To Sender' and 'Jailhouse Rock') briefly returned to the chart, 'Way Down'

moved to Number One for five weeks (Elvis's first chart-topper for seven years), and eleven LPs were listed.

The day after he died, Elvis's body was put on display at Graceland, where 20,000 mourners filed past the open coffin. On 18 August, Elvis was buried in Forest Hills Cemetery after a funeral at Graceland, where over 3,000 floral tributes were sent. While Vernon, Priscilla and Lisa-Marie sat in the front row, Tom Parker was at the back of the room in his shirtsleeves. He had

'Nothing has changed. This won't change anything. We must immediately make sure that outsiders cannot exploit the name of Elvis Presley.'
COLONEL PARKER AFTER ELVIS'S DEATH

already negotiated a merchandising deal that guaranteed $150,000 plus a royalty on every sale of Presley paraphernalia, half going to Parker himself and the other half being divided between his company, Boxcar Enterprises, and the Presley estate. It must be stressed that nothing Parker did while he

'The best career move he's made in years.'
ANONYMOUS CRITIC ON THE DEATH OF ELVIS

was managing Elvis was illegal; he merely proved himself an incredible opportunist.

Some time later a television show conducted an investigation into the real cause of Presley's death, and the general view was that his heart attack, far from being natural, was provoked by polypharmacy, a combination of a variety of different drugs, which is consistent with the suggestions in the books by the West brothers and Hebler. Before

---

'It's still Elvis and the Colonel, but now it's Elvis and Vernon Presley and the Colonel. Elvis didn't die, the body did. We're keeping up our spirits and keeping Elvis alive. I talked to him this morning and he told me to carry on.'

COLONEL PARKER

---

the end of 1973 a new double album, *Elvis In Concert*, was released, which included material recorded at a concert in Omaha, Nebraska, less than two months before he died. Biographers have called the sound of Elvis's voice 'a death rattle', and it is widely believed that had he survived, the album would almost certainly have been at least delayed, if not scrapped altogether.

The Elvis industry continued unabated, perhaps benefiting from a lengthy biography by New York writer Albert Goldman, which sold prodigiously but was reviled by rock critics. It destroyed the Elvis myth in far too convincing a manner for those who had found him an inspiration, and appeared equally scathing about his admirers. The general criticism was that because Goldman was obviously not a great fan of Elvis, his arguments about Elvis being despicable, even if true, should have been balanced by some appreciation of his talent. The important thing as far as Colonel Parker was concerned was that the name of Elvis was back in the headlines, which was inevitably good for business. Elvis still tops the lists of US chart achievements in every category – most hits, most in the top forty, most in the top ten, most Number One hits, most consecutive Number Ones and most consecutive Top Ten hits. What he could have achieved with greater consistency, sympathetic management and somebody answering him back, we can only imagine.

LEFT: *Faithful fans and friends still pay tribute to Elvis by his grave in Forest Hills Cemetery.*